THE LEAVES ARE TURNING

A BOOK OF POEMS

MOG P.

Made with ♥ on the Notion Press Platform
www.notionpress.com

Contents

Contents

Contents

For my family

1. Once upon a Monsoon Night

In the dark stillness of this monsoon night,
it is not raining,
and I can hear
the roar of the distant sea
foaming and seething and singing to the dark clouds—
just out of reach,
teasing them to abandon themselves.

And there she comes, the rain –
A fine veil of sound that shrouds
all the mysterious voices of this night—
the croaking and creaking and chirping of things.
Slowly she comes, then builds into
a fleeting crescendo
that crashes upon the roof, then
eases and echoes
until all is still again and,
I can hear the delicate pings
of the dripping water, she left behind.

2. Rebirth of a Lily

Blood Lily!
What a frightful name!
A farce,
that I find is far far from the truth.
For the blood lily is not red,
but orange—
A bulbous sparkler of petals
ignited by the first rains.
Glory to thee,
Oh magnanimous monsoon!

Blood Lily,
I'd like to rechristen thee—
Sun Lily.
A sun, erupted from the depths of a playful earth
who teases her children with this
ball of pseudo fire,
now that her grey friends have reunited
to block out the sun and drown her in mirth.

Oh charming Sun Lily,
of my childhood,
of my youth, now fading.

Please choose to forgive our crimes
and continue to rise for us,
on your annual circuit through the earth,
for me, my children and theirs.

3. Ode to the Old Mango Tree

Gibbous green fruit,
you glisten in the sun,
hiding, shy within your mother's green skirts
while she cradles you with pride-
her finest accomplishment,
her phoenix-egg.

When that rain-shot storm came,
and ripped her apart from limb to limb,
she stood courageously still.
Thereafter, weeping and shivering in its hot aftermath.
'Tsk tsk tsk', I had thought, 'she will never recover,
poor thing!'

But here you are, plump and glazed—
The sole heir this year,
to a once fertile mother.
Why! I can't wait to see
how much she surprises me the next season.
The valiant old tree,
that has inspired me so!

4. The anti-gods of inertia have colonised the roof

This house, it stands old and thick
with its ancient sloping roof-
baked red tiles, all of them,
with their burnt backs to the sky
and all the elements, but one-
The anti-gods of inertia.
A whole colony of them,
countless and brazen,
running amok and unhindered
o'er that high, out-of-reach ceiling.

They cause delight and disdain,
such two-faced creatures,
whose name has come to embody mischief.
Squirrel away, squirrel away,
at every change of day,
and pass the night in mocking, twitching stillness,
then chirp loudly to greet the breaking light,
shove us out of sweet slumber,
and then, squirrel away, squirrel away.

5. Golden fountain tree

T'is February and I see that
the golden fountain
is alive and overflowing,
brimming with pale yellow light,
working hard to compensate
for all those months
it didn't move, didn't contribute,
didn't shine-
-just stood there dull and content,
forced by the hand of creation
into wistful waiting—
waiting for February—
to burst into dazzling flame,
to reflect the glory of the sun,
until the mighty hand can turn it off again.
As if such peerless beauty
needs to be rationed, in order
to be savoured.

6. The coconut plucker, the kites and the coconut tree

Damu hitched up his shorts
and glanced up.
The narrow grey trunk beckoned,
swaying ever so gently.
Its green canopy, carefree, whistled breezily
to edge him on.
He hugged her, the tree, idly,
without fear or trepidation.
As he scaled her lithely,
his thoughts wandered off to the skies.
Really! This was no trouble at all—
Just another day on the job.

He was midway up
when he heard the haunted heavy cries
of a pair of kites
as they encircled him, hissing and cursing.
Two strong pairs of lush feathered wings
flapped the air and made it sing.
All at once, he was scared.

Was this how it felt to be scooped up by angels?
But these were no gentle spirits—
Two hooked beaks and twelve gilded talons
all trained at his flesh,
Two sets of accusing dark eyes bore into his,
And all the while, their menacing cries.

He clung to her, the tree, for dear life.
She swayed unhindered, nonchalant.
If he climbed any higher,
the pair would only draw nearer,
weapons drawn and poised to kill.
The uneventful day had turned on him.
His courage broke,
His grip on her loosened
and he began his gradual shameful descent.
The warrior pair disengaged.
When Damu's feet shakily touched the ground,
he looked up scratching his head in dismay.
The deceptive canopy had kept,
her secret well,
and the little fledgling darlings, safe in their nest.

7. The Amado tree

A beautiful, lush Amado tree
stood in our garden, but two days ago.
I loved that peridot canopy which
turned the golden sunlight, green,
bore tender, pale fruit
and matured them into swollen seed.
Over the years, we planted an incorrigible climber
that wrapped itself around our tree like a veil
and from its fringes swung dainty purple bells
that rang in schools of beautiful winged creatures
into its breezy halls-
Red-rumped bulbuls, and yellow,
jittery rainbow sunbirds, black and white magpie robins,
and others which I cannot name.
Our tree, such a comfortable, looming presence,
a safe haven for life, for song, and for thought—
the object of my admiration, a companion in solitude,
an inhibitor of nervous energy, and
a filter of the anxiety oft brought on
by the brutal rashness of this fast world.
Why then, did you let it come apart?
When there are so many undeserving things, still standing?
Oh, how I miss my gentle tree!

8. About the vine of purple flowers

The vine of purple flowers
shrouds the tree like a thick veil.
Its flowering tassels swing gently in the breeze
offering crimson sunbirds,
gentle cups of sweetness.

9. Earth-bound angels

Oh, all ye faithful! You wait for heavenly angels to show,
but fail to see,
what God would have you know—
that the custodians of wings in the air
and fins 'neath the sea,
in this life, what better angels could there be?

10. Butterfly aristocracy

The Holy Blue and the Common Yellow,
together in a flowery bed.
Shed their titles and fed.

11. Imagine autumn

Imagine autumn,
when leaves float down,
in rich tones of oranges and reds,
like so many monarchs, falling from grace.

12. Bougainvillea

The pink bougainvillea is widespread evidence
of the marriage between sun and rain.
A vibrant and sturdy wedding band,
prickly to those who dare interfere
as if to bid them
to forever hold their peace.

13. Outside my office window

I am grateful for the green lights
that twinkle at the corner of my eye,
and pull my eyes into comfort.
I am grateful for the bejewelled being
who catches sun beams for fun
and tosses them over to me
in glowing peridot, emerald and gold.
How lovely it is to sit here and be
and have outside my window, a Peepal tree.

I turn my head to gaze at thee,
thy shapely leaves with bold midribs seen,
thy love of dancing in the breeze
and making peaceful music.
And when my mind's peace has been stolen,
anxiety and anger raise their heads to strike,
all I need to do is look at thee
in thy perfect contentment.
How lovely it is to sit here and be
and have outside my window, a Peepal tree.

14. Baby Banyan in hotel foyer

Oh how they have bedecked you!
You with olivine leaf and rich mist root,
Green anthuriums at your concrete-clad feet
stick their tongues out at those
who dare to gaze upon your splendour.
Wild white pilgrims flutter
through your boughs,
bold squirrels scurry through your shade,
glass lanterns suspended from chains
dangle from your arms,
while your roots clutch the air
with nowhere to strike
but an unyielding concrete floor.
They have got you trapped, haven't they?
A proud, bejewelled, reluctant bride
with nowhere to grow.

15. Cashew grove

The keepers of the cashew grove
hold court beneath its leafy boughs,
twisting apple from its seed,
for the apple plump with juice divine
and the seed, pinched, bent and heaven sent.

16. The forest vine

There is no stillness in you,
Ye sturdy vine—
Stretch, reach, unfurl, entwine,
capture a branch.
Stretch, reach, unfurl, entwine,
capture the next one up…
and again,
and again,
and again,
until you've swallowed a living tree
into your dark menacing belly.
Then, onto the next—
A forest engulfed.
Shall I be the hand of God?
Find your roots
and snip…
and grant perhaps the one thing you crave
that's true,
Rest at last!
In death.

17. Lose the feathers!

With the unclaimed sacrifices of old,
we have feathered shallow nests—
mere tools of fleeting comfort.
We have traded our vision
for rosy, branded sunglasses
which will lose relevance in time.
We have become selfish and dangerous
toying with the future,
out on a ledge, soon to have it slip and shatter.
Stop it! Right now!
Honour the past,
Gather your vision to yourself
like a precious warm garb on a cold night,
so that the future is not lost to the barren winter.

18. Windblown

Here upon this purple night,
the lone windblown tower
at center still
stranded aloft the abandoned hill,
the light in streaks,
the current strong,
the stone will resist…
but for how long?
As if it forgets to bend,
refusing help,
refusing to mend
the furrow that runs
along its side—
Testament to an unfair tide,
when it rained all night
and washed off shine.
It hid the hope
and blurred the line.
Hence trust was lost,
a faith had fumbled,
a life had lived,
but at what cost?

19. Still Waters

There are times when my life resembles turbulent waters.
Yet, after the wind and the rain
have taken their toll with God's blessings,
calmness and peace engulfs the tides again
and the waters mix with serenity
like a divine concoction.
But God loves to play the waters of my peaceful lake.
He picks up a heavy pebble,
hurls it into still waters,
and sadistically smiles as the ripples unfold.

I can do nothing.
I am at the master's mercy.
Of his sport, I pray he may tire,
or that pebbles cease to exist.
But they are omnipresent,
being churned continuously by the water's bed.
I know of lakes,
which wear with pride, the hues that ripples bring.
I am not of kin.

Does my master know me
as I wish he would?

If so, why doesn't he just let me be?
He disturbs my silence
and confuses my tide.
I am but a mere weakling, my Lord.
Test me not, and be my guide.

20. Learn Loneliness

Your canvass may be immersed in colour,
blending in harmony
to gloat a picture of perfection—
the joy of celebration,
the comfort received in sorrow,
the faces to nestle amidst
in summer's glory.
Yet, even now,
when all is warm and alive,
Learn loneliness.

Make peace with silence,
have a tear part a smile.
For when skies go dark
and smiles melt into gloom,
faces fade into the fray,
and loneliness draws happiness
into an inert vacuum.

When flesh longs to be caressed,
and the voice yearns to be heard,
and the heart craves to love,
the peace that hails within the soul

is not promised to silence.
At times their union remains unblessed
whilst turmoil seizes the soul.

When the limelight glitters upon another
and you lay awake in the shadows,
do not let life disown you.
For when misery sheds its skin
one emerges stronger still.
If the past has taken companions for granted,
the future never will.

21. Shifting sands

I have dreamt in shattered whispers,
and now I stand on a sand dune
whilst the sands shift beneath my feet.
I have been held and lead through early life
and have complied for duty and want,
and now I stand on a sand dune,
whilst the sands shift beneath my feet.
I have believed in signs
and craved divine intervention,
and wondered about greatness and glory,
and now I stand on a sand dune,
whilst the sands shift beneath my feet.

But now, I walk on playful knolls
clutching at the wind, to find a pillar,
sinking into the sand, up to my calves.
The caring hands that once held me
now gently push through uneasy shores.
The divine is a light on the edge of the horizon,
and the signs lie buried deep in the sand.
And I still dream in shattered whispers,
with the wind howling in my ears,
proclaiming a whole new life.

22. A Prayer

A prayer is…
what calms the violent storm
that rages within one's soul.
It is the soft medicine
that heals the wound inflicted
by the cruel blow of love's hand.
Even if we call out to the father,
only when the shrill winds announce
the coming of a tempest,
you might think that the thunder will muffle
the sound of your weak trembling voice.
Yet, he hears you.
Your voice becomes his knife
piercing through vast sediments of noise.

Even if it has been very long
since he last heard you,
he recognises you distinctly
amidst the chaos of cries which rise up to him.
He is always listening.
He has patience enough to fill
the vast vacuum, that is the universe.
Even while you pour out your heart to him,

his touch can soothe.
The strength of his arms
can lift any load off your shoulders.
He forgives.
He gives.
He frees your spirit,
and all he asks in return,
is to hear the sound of your voice more often.

23. Worn shores

A bowl of dust cupping the floor,
a pair of eyes fixed on the door.
All the monotony,
the bitter embrace,
the jaded will,
that is no more.
I cannot explain.
The reason has left without a trace.
Its return would bring me no relief,
in its loss, I feel no grief.
Let it be.

As times move by, peace will rest,
nostalgic senses will receive the best.
The sea will mourn her son.
He will be born again
and lose himself in her love.
Her breath will glow,
lavender grief,
red furry,
pink hope,
whilst tears wash up on her worn shores.
But he will be born again—

the star in her life,
the quest in mine.

24. Dreams

Sweet dreams are made of the unattained.
Extraordinary events
can spring from the mundane.
Emotion can blossom and overstep
into the surreal.
Beware pretty novice!
This is unchartered territory.
But you have been here before,
a long time ago.
I had hoped that you weren't as naïve
any more,
but here you are, yet again.
Do not commit to the vicarious!
Life will not bless the union.
Wake up and realize!
Novelty must be lived,
not dreamt.

25. Sounds of the night

I have stilled my flickering box of a companion
for a moment,
to listen to the sounds of the night.
Broken music from a neighbour's open window
cuts through the walls and closed panes.
My neighbour who loves music,
and better still, loves to sing,
joins the electronic voice on the chorus.
Then,
the intermittent sounds of engines
dying for the night,
the steady ticking of the clock,
and deeper still, the incessant fiddling
of the cricket.
Ah! These are the sounds of the night,
before I turn my TV back on
and flick over to the next channel.

26. Standing

I've seen the face of guilt.
I've seen it in my mirror
standing at the foot of my bed, greeting
every noon I rise to,
contemptuous of the late hour I choose,
forever flaunting taunts with eagerness
at my lethargic dreams,
my incomplete faith,
my blatant disregard,
the lack of myself!
The list I perceive is long
and unending,
too long to reform, I daresay,
too deep to recover
from sunken depths, wherever those may
lead to.
A simple day is all it needs,
ordinary in every sense—
a day guarded against solitary thought,
enough to let the night run its charm
into morning,
and face but an ordinary mirror,
standing, at the foot of my bed.

27. Ashes and Dust

I died today.
I died when I was born into a world
completely alien to me.
A world that held me, not by will or desire,
A world so dull, it didn't inspire.
And yet this land so barren to me,
is a green oasis to the eyes of many a traveller.
But I sit on the hard dead ground,
my hand weary from clutching the ashes of my true calling.
Funny though,
I wonder,
How could there be ashes,
when there was nothing to burn?
I don't think that I deserve such a fate,
even if I wasn't sincere enough.
The hope I need to keep me going,
seems to be a glittering star, galaxies away.
I don't think that I can bear the pain
As I lie in wait on the dusty plain.

28. On an empty heart and stomach

I feel empty. It's a void that has expanded
and the vacuum that is pressing against my chest,
has all vitality on the brink of collapse.
I cannot use food to fill me anymore.
It's a new regime, and my stomach throbs with craving.
There will be no warm bread with pungent trimmings,
no rich creams and dark heavy chocolate.
Now there is only emptiness
and along with it, despair.

My world is missing something.
I shall be sure of what, only once I find it.
The spirit has fallen prey to my lack of faith.
There is no more inspiration and no more purpose.
Novelty is a fleeting comfort
and in my case, it is long gone.

Sound out like a church bell in distress,
Oh my empty heart!
Call out for a saviour who may never come.
Relearn your old lessons on survival and
unlearn those that only fuel your desolation.

Let the bell ring out loud and clear
for all to hear!!

29. Cupid's sting

Love, sweetly poisoned
to taste like nectar from the angels,
But like a drug that swindles
its way through blood
and holds the heart prisoner,
is, in the end lethal too.
Those prized words…
…I love you.

30. The Moment

There was nothing I could do,
There was no one I could turn to.
I was alone.
The front of my mind
was being swept
by ghosts scurrying to get to salvation.
The moment was filled with silence,
The sky was never so blue,
but my words were hollow
and unimportant all through.
I was not able to endorse the moment.

The silence so demanding,
drained me of all my energy.
Was it stubbornness that had triumphed?
Or, was it a mimosian style of shyness?
What was the urgency I was feeling?
Had I known it before?
Did it have a name?
For it continues to prey on my honour,
and to laugh at my face.

31. Foreigner

Seeing him again, brought back old memories, and awakened emotion.
Oh God! I thought that I had forgotten.
But after half a decade, I felt again.
I thought that the vacuum, I usually live in,
had stabilised my life.
But one meeting with him, and the seal was broken.
As the air and moisture gushed in, I felt myself swell
in that secret kind of joy, that only a stimulated heart can bring.
But I know like the previous times, that I cannot have this man.
There is a lot of circumstance standing in our way again
and I have not the courage to overcome or try.
It seems wrong to try,
and I will not wage war with my conscience.
I will endure in silence, until the turbulence in my spirit ceases
and the distance that is the natural barrier between him and I
drains my heart and reseals its space.
And I will hope and pray for a different encounter
and a different man, to break the seal, and fill my heart,
and maybe finally, hold my hand.

32. The One

Dear Lord,
Is he the one for me?
I need a sign of courage,
for intuition has betrayed me
and my poor heart is failing in impulse.
It lacks the strength to direct me.
I am not ready to lose him
even though I thought that I had convinced myself.
It seems that my masquerade was weak
and shabby
for I liked him even when I disliked him.
I am confused by his lack of initiative,
hurt, that he cares no more than a friend,
haunted by my own doubts and impressions,
frightened by my own deficiencies.
I don't know if he is the one for me,
but I know that I am not ready
to lose him.

33. Hopeless

I am beginning to find it
ever so hopeless.
I do not want
to chain hope to my chair
or twist it into a convenient shape
upon my ring finger.
I can tell you,
what it feels like to be disappointed..
to simply count the colours of the rainbow,
Waiting for it to pass,
just to look out for the next,
and hope…
yet again.

34. Island

Am I alone on my island?
I always see the new couple next door.
I always look,
I always smile
to myself.
Love seems to have found them
in their element.
I always wonder,
but wish cautiously enough,
to know Love.
How does that happen anyway?
I know of infatuation,
I have tasted sweet agony,
but Love eludes me.
Is it inspiring? Is it a commitment?
Or an ephemeral wonder, in need
of constant gratification?
Is it fear that prompts doubt?
Not of not knowing love,
but of not recognizing it at the right instant.
Am I alone on my island?

35. Unrequited

Uneasy affection,
Fickle sentiment unable to hold,
its claim on good intention.
Hidden glances yearning surrender,
all part of a Venus that is Love.

He was in Love.
Spared no tenderness in expression,
yearned for returns that would never come.
Yet, now his heart deserted
is haunted by an ageing ghost.

Seated beside her, he listens
to her heart, as it speaks of someone else.
His own makes not a sound,
but for its beat,
that just lost its rhythm.

36. Sour Fruit

There was once a deep void in his heart.
The flesh was tender still.
But she had gentle hands,
a soothing touch,
a stronger will.
She placed a seed in it.
That seed, he did not understand
and knew little of its origin or its end.
She nursed it with her patience.
Reluctantly, he did with bitter tears.
From it sprung a forest
that smelt of fresh jasmine
and bore sour fruit…
with the sweetness of her love
and the bitterness of his ache.
He finds the flavor intriguing
and savours its texture.
He offers her a piece,
She smiles, she has done her part
and now,
she has just been offered
the fruit borne of his heart.

37. Blue Man

He lives in my world.
Yet, he loves only in my dreams.
I speak of him, in my wide-eyed slumber,
of his gentle ways,
his wide smile
and humble intelligence,
of his music.

My words never reach him,
my sights always find him,
almost.
Yet my heart is tied to
the wings of a humming bird,
humming the song of a smolt
that must soon leave its creek.

I know him, but I don't.
I want to love him, but I won't...
I have not yet seen the colours of his soul.
Although,
I have dipped my finger in his presence—
It feels soft and tender, like the sky –
A sky that's always blue,

almost.

Blue man,
You invite wonder.
Have you seen it in my eyes?

38. The Party

Words that are used to a poet,
have promised to make simple sense.
It has been the beginning to feelings,
earlier acquaintances,
now my closest friends…
by way of a mutual stranger.

I don't recall where it started
or how, or why?
I have only come to see
the strength of his presence.
Let me share my night of music
and dance…
His shyness
that left me in wonder
and in prayer.

Dancing, this night,
did more than satisfy me,
it needed to impress him.
It barely succeeded.
Then my feet grew weary
and I nearly twisted my heart

on the dance floor.

They changed the lovely rhythm
and he rushed to help them
as if he had perhaps hoped.
I acknowledged thirst
and agreed to quench,
Water and cold-drink refreshed…
me and the lovely rhythm.
He stood alone, again,
shy on the dance floor.

A new determination:
"May I?"
It was me.
And in a while,
it was me and him,
and a song, that is slowly becoming
A favourite.

39. Night

If I am the moon,
Then, you are my night.
I cling to your darkness
which devoid of any star
lasts eternal.

40. Puppy

Do you want to be his puppy?
Or wait till your heart outgrows him?
Admit it! You love the sweetness,
you have, for the first time, tasted in pain.
Do you want to wage war on emotion?
and have yourself condemned
for a sentimental fool?
Does his hidden smile reveal your secret?
Or is it just a cruel joke of the imagination?
Perhaps yours.
Perhaps his.
Are you ready to burn in a love,
handed from the torch of infatuation?
But first,
do you accept your mad disposition?
and the incredulous fact
that he doesn't even know
or doesn't want to?

41. Roaming

I love roaming the sky.
I love trying to reach it
and nearly succeeding.
I wonder about its inconsistency,
and I love the way
it feeds my day with
some of its magic—
Having every moment
occur in a different shade of blue.

Every once in a while,
A white cloud catches my eye
and reaches for my heart.
But I politely draw back.
I am bound to.
It is forbidden to live in the clouds.
It might as well be.
The clouds are adrift,
but the sky will always stay.

I love roaming the sky,
It is beautiful, and it is silent.
I love roaming the sky,

It has not yet been said,
that I love the sky.

42. Confrontation

Do you want me to apologize to the world,
for the flaws which make me who I am?
Is the price of living, life itself?
Then, why take away my sunshine,
when the night is under your spell?
Why rob me of the story,
before it can live, before I can tell?
And why oh why?
Tickle my heart,
make it swell, to let dwell.
But tune it to alternate
between yearning and gratification.
Why never let love stray from its shadow?
Is the price of loving, love itself?
Is the price of living, life itself?

43. Moving On

You did not notice,
you did not say anything to me,
you have the gift of silence.
I can never tell if you even think of me again
after one of the rare times when we meet.
I reciprocate with silence.
I have my pride.
But even a single encounter,
after so many months of silence
makes me restless.
My imagination sends ripples
through my memories of you,
resurrects hope in a situation
that I have so often deemed hopeless.
Like the gentlest breeze that blows
through tender branches
and makes music with the leaves,
it feels so natural.

I should give up on you,
or, take the first step in your direction.
Which is the easier of the two?
I cannot seem to find the courage for either.

Please help me...
Notice me, tell me how you feel, even break my heart.
But put an end to the silence,
to the unfounded hopes
and let me move on.

44. Together

Does love completely go away?
I'd like to think not,
It just dims, covered by the soot and grime
of little jealousies, resentments and
a great many things left unsaid—
You would think that you saved yourselves
from a petty quarrel,
But that restless thing will stay with you
and prick you every now and then.
Better to say what you feel,
Better to strip an issue bare
until it has no place to hide.
Then, pick your coat off the floor
and together look for the bones of your ballad
and bring it back home.

45. The Bystander

The wind whips the reeds into a frenzy
and blows stray leaves from their nodes.
She too has come undone
and struggles to find her balance.
She stares in his direction
but there hand in pocket he stands, upright,
A bystander to her plight.

How soon a memory it becomes, that time
when his hand was warm around hers
and the love in her heart felt warm and bright.
But there were promises made,
long before their own,
that are his to keep and his to break.
And to her it seems that,
he has made his choice,
as her hands grow cold and
her heart grows dim
with the faded promise of him.

46. The End of Love

The End of Love
Is like the beginning of a lesser life.
There is no doubt that something's gone missing—
some vital part of you.

Sound the horn! The hunt begins
in terrains of old and new,
Charge your steed into recklessness
or rein it into a cautious trot
and wonder,
if time is foe or friend.

I will survive!
I will be whole again!

47. Vicarious

I search, search, sift, sift,
through layers and layers of content
for that spark
to reignite an old flame, now in embers.
Ah! That bright, burning flame
which consumed all in its path—
Reality, duty, sense and all.
And I, mad, march towards self-immolation,
Like a hapless moth
flung into the fire by basic instinct.
Indeed! Tempting death, just to feel alive.

48. Mermaid's whim

I don't feel like writing.
The jar is getting empty.
The fingers are weary,
The mind has wandered
into the sea
so vast,
turquoise,
white foam,
graceful and brutal.

I listened to her whisper,
straining for the sweetness
of an elusive song,
to catch it from a mermaid
tucked safely within a fluid bosom.

The mermaid,
I need her.
She has what is mine.
She wears it on a string around her neck.
It is a fickle whim to her,
But a precious gift to me!
The jar feels empty! Already!

49. To the Artist

Trying to lure the intricate forms,
moulded by skin on paper
needs the strength of discerning vision
and equal weakness of sensitive touch.
For the marriage between flesh and bone,
bears skin, which may belie character,
every pore of which
traps and reflects light,
in a manner that is unique to itself.

50. New Year's Eve

Today, it's New Year's Eve.
Tonight there will be music, and dancing , and wine,
and tomorrow, life will go on as usual.
Just time, staking its claim
over our mortal lives, once again.

I am home for the season
and have to leave again.
My moments have been haunted by time.
I don't want to close my eyes
on every day that passes me by
and brings me closer to the loneliness
that is my other life.

People prepare for their night of folly
and the spirit is contagious,
it almost makes me not recall
the myriad issues that vex my thoughts,
The variety of monsters, my mind conjures up
to hurl at its own sanity.

Let the festivities move on,
let people for one night, forget the day tomorrow

and pretend to change their lives
for the new year ahead.
Let us sway to the music
and slay all our demons for the night,
and not think of tomorrow's tomorrow.
Let it just be New Year's Eve
and let nothing else matter.

51. College friends

I remember the first day, I walked into the new classroom.
Almost every face, a new one,
almost every look, a strange one.
I could feel sad memories of the happy past
loom in my mind,
but here I was in a very real present
with a reality of the worst kind.
I felt like an alien in a totally strange land,
where even if I spoke, no one would understand.

But now my friend, when we are forced to part,
I realise how very wrongly I felt at the start.
Yes, I admit, it took us a few days,
to get to know each other,
even to smile at the other.
But when the strange looks melted into smiles,
and when the solemn emptiness between us
was filled with the warmth of friendship,
the winds of uncertainty blew away,
and I began to cherish each and every day.
I still do.
It was and still is because of you.

Perhaps we will not see each other again,
If we're lucky, we'll meet along the way.
I wish you all the very best life can offer.
Please remember,
your friendship means a lot to me,
no matter where life leads us…
..Good friends, we'll always be.

52. Remembering Iggy (Ignatius)

I found Iggy again
tucked amidst my favourite poems,
A sweet memory who swims to my surface
every once in a while.
'Who is Iggy?'
Should you ask—
--Well, Iggy was an old man
with the aura of a young boy,
soundly forgotten in a home for the elderly.
He must have once been somebody's favourite uncle, perhaps.
For I could not picture him
as somebody's father.
That boyish imp, poor old urchin!

He spent his days cutting out
shapes in cards—
Mementos to anyone who cared,
presented with delicate papery hands
and the crackling of a high voice.
(I could almost hear the teenage angst in it.)
A visit later, he was gone,
along with my chance to say goodbye.

And so, I made him a sweet memory
who swims to my surface,
every time I find the cut-out of the Christmas card
he once gave me,
tucked safely amongst precious poems,
which will never die
and keep his memory alive,
while at it.

53. Children of God

Waves of little children all decked in white,
are arranged in neat honourable rows,
with white flowers in satin and pearl
piled high on little heads,
overflowing with veils.
Groomed white candles, bob
above the foamy fray.
Below, little feet tap and fidget.
Here are the blessed, God's delight,
his train of dreams
as they sit together in all innocence
expectant and open to his grace.

54. Bakhita's smile on her First Holy Communion day

Bakhita's smile was radiant,
she was beautiful.
Her joy was pure and complete,
a child's joy, but much more.
Surely it is a gift. Such a pure expression of joy
that reached out to me
and pulled me into its rapture.
And I keep thinking
how unselfish it is
to spill over and fill someone else,
with even a momentary reminder of God's love.
Like Bakhita's smile did.
Keep smiling, little angel.

55. The visit to the lotus pond

I took my little boy to the lotus pond
of pale pink, bouncy and bulbous delights,
like sweet cotton candy
spun on tall stems.
We watched as dragon flies
wearing yellow and green stripes
dashed amidst wayward petals
in precise sorties.
Perfect green discs,
like outlandish serving platters
laid out an enviable spread.

'Are there fish? Are they hiding?
Do they miss the sun?'
Yes, my son, they hide, but live content
in a world as big as our own,
green canopied and complex,
teeming with more life
than we care to imagine.
What meets the eye, are candied delights.
But the real opulence lies in the world beneath.

56. Baby girl

My baby girl,
I have dressed you today
in a slushy pink t-shirt
with four white stripes,
and I think of how sweet you are,
and of how much I love having you.
When the doctor held you up,
I was filled with the joy of you,
the love of you,
and a gratitude for you
that has since made me a better person.
Your helpless infancy did not tire me,
for this type of love, I find, is inexhaustible.
I know that someday,
you will find me exhausting.
You will tell me to leave you alone,
and being who I am, I probably will.
But though I may be away from you,
I will never be apart, from the part of me,
that is you.

57. The precious burn

I carelessly scorched my wrist
on a kitchen flame,
and had my skin bubble
into a malicious balloon.
Three days passed
and it subsided
into a maroon mark of ineptitude
as if marked by a teacher's angry red pen.
Then, my little darling came along
and exclaimed, "Mama, booboo!"
"Torry", she lisped
and kissed the spot loudly,
and turned a thoughtless blunder
into a badge of honour.

58. Home

This temperate place,
of perennial sun,
where the sky is unabashedly emotional
and winter, but a whisper to behold.

I call this heat my passion,
These tears my soul,
These fleeting cool kisses, my aspirations,
This enduring warmth, my home.

59. Susegado

Susegado:
a most romantic way of life.
You do not need to run a race and chase life
to prove that you have lived it.
Sometimes, if you let life come to you
and welcome it without reservation,
you will have lived it, just as well
maybe even better.

60. Oh, land of my heart!

Oh, land of my heart, of my soul,
my pride, my refuge, my home.
I clutch to my heart my memories of you,
I wince in pain at your turning plight.
I hide in my indifference to your ghastly wounds,
to free my unkempt mind.
But all the while I am quietly burning in my
possessiveness of you,
until my mind plies my restless thoughts
with beautiful ideas
which only fall prey to my tired passiveness.
Despite all of my flaws, my cowardice
and inaction,
I know you will still forgive me
and cradle my grave at my life's end.

www.ingramcontent.com/pod-product-compliance
Lightning Source LLC
LaVergne TN
LVHW021200160826
845679LV00024B/2190

* 9 7 9 8 8 9 1 8 6 3 1 0 1 *